C000321358

'Riveting, powerful,
stories of the grace
Lindsay Brown, *For*
former Internationa

'These are stories the world needs to hear and Christians need to know. Don Cormack knew and loved and served so many of these brothers and sisters, who loved Jesus more than life itself. With depth and compassion he brings us their voices first-hand, tracing the beautiful fruit borne out of the killing fields.'

Mark Ellis, *CEO, Keswick Ministries*

'There is a kind of suffering so heinous, it is beyond telling. Yet when Christ's redemptive grace floods the scene, that same suffering takes on an exalted glow of glory. It's what I experienced in reading these powerful stories. Be blessed as you read them, letting them whet your appetite for the larger classic work from which they are drawn.'

Joni Eareckson Tada, *Joni and Friends International Disability Center*

'Convicting, inspiring and sobering. These stories pierced my soul. Let your heart, spirit and mind be moved as you read of those who did not count the cost of what it means to follow Jesus.'

Sarah Breuel, *Director of Revive Europe; Member, Lausanne Movement Board*

ABOUT THE AUTHOR

Don Cormack served with OMF International in Malaysia, Taiwan, Cambodia, Thailand and Singapore from 1972-1996.

After being forced to flee from Cambodia in 1975, he worked in Cambodian refugee camps along the Thai/Cambodian border. He also taught at the Discipleship Training Centre and ministered to heroin addicts in Singapore, before returning to Cambodia in 1992, following the signing of the Paris Peace Accords. He was ordained by the Bishop of Singapore to begin the Church of Christ our Peace, in Phnom Penh.

Don married Margaret Lockhart at Chefoo School in 1979. They have three adult daughters. After returning to the UK, he completed his award-winning book: *Killing Fields, Living Fields*, now in its eighth edition, which chronicles the Cambodian church from its beginnings in the 1920s to the present day.

TEN STORIES
FROM THE
KILLING FIELDS

dictumpress.com

Copyright © Don Cormack

First published in this form by OMF International, 1999,
reprinted 2000.

First Dictum Edition (Expanded and updated) 2024

ISBN 978-1-8380972-9-5
EPub ISBN 978-1-915934-22-2

Taken from *Killing Fields, Living Fields* by Don Cormack
Dictum edition 2024
ISBN 978-1-8380972-3-3
EPub ISBN 978-1-915934-23-9

Scripture verses taken from the Revised Standard Version of
the Bible.

Design - Chris Gander and Pete Barnsley

Published by Dictum Press, Oxford, UK *dictumpress.com*

TEN STORIES
FROM THE
KILLING FIELDS
Don Cormack

In partnership with OMF International

AUTHOR'S DEDICATION

I dedicate this small book to a great cloud of witnesses, to the thousands of Cambodian Christians who perished in Pol Pot's killing fields between 1975 and 1979. Many were young people and students. They lie in unmarked mass graves all across the land.

Let us be mindful, too, of legions of others across the world, including children, who, even now, are being persecuted and killed in the most brutal ways imaginable — faithful unto death.

The world is not worthy of them. They will receive the crown of righteousness.

CONTENTS

About the author   ii

Map   6

Foreword by Julia Cameron   7

PART 1: SETTING THE SCENE

The flight from Phnom Penh   19

The fall of Phnom Penh   25

PART 2: COMPELLING STORIES

1. Van Rean's story   37

2. Chen's story 'How beautiful are the feet'   39

3. Events on the third anniversary   43

4. Pastor Reach Yeah   47

5. Haim and his family face their execution   57

6. Christmas!   61

7. Pastor Hom, his flock, and his personal grief   69

8. A boy whose brother is dying   77

9. A Khmer Rouge soldier finds forgiveness   81

10. A mother's love   85

Afterword   91

Timeline   97

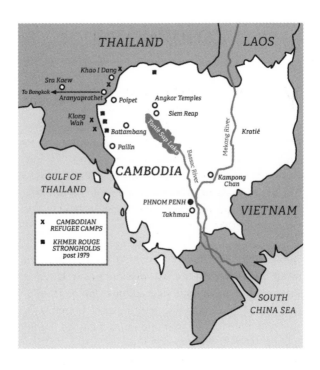

Author's note: The word Khmer is virtually synonymous with Cambodian, since 96% of Cambodians are ethnic Khmers, as opposed to Chinese, or other minorities.

FOREWORD

You are about to read some remarkable stories. They will stay with you. I'm sure of that.

Don Cormack's *Killing Fields, Living Fields*, from which these excerpts are taken, traces the journey of the Cambodian church from its early beginnings among a few Battambang rice farmers in the 1920s, through to the present day. We hope these vignettes may make you want to read more.

Don Cormack is uniquely qualified to tell Cambodia's story. He was one of the last missionaries to leave Phnom Penh when it fell to the Khmer Rouge in 1975, and one of the first to return afterwards. In between, he spent time in the sprawling refugee camps which sprang up along the Thai/Cambodian border. Don learned the Cambodian language, and his pastoral approach won the trust of those he met. Some were deeply traumatized, and could tell him their stories only a little at a time, over weeks or months.

These cameos convey something of Cambodia's tragic history between 1975 & 1979, when little news was coming out of the country. In that small southeast Asian nation, through darkness, and bloodshed, and fear, and sheer evil, we trace the hand of God. There has been unimaginable cruelty in many other parts of the world, and one wonders how similar the experiences of Christians have been in these places.

BEING A CHRISTIAN MADE YOU A PARIAH

It took 1900 years for the gospel to reach the Khmer people. When David Ellison, an American missionary, first gave a copy of Luke's gospel to some simple Cambodian rice farmers in 1923, they were riveted. The truth took hold of their hearts. In such a deeply Buddhist culture, Christian believers were shunned, despised and vulnerable. They were sometimes imprisoned, and always blamed when there was sickness or crop-failure in a village. Being a Christian made you a pariah.

Fifty years later, shortly before Pol Pot came to power, the Holy Spirit began to move in new ways. While threatening clouds were gathering over Cambodia in 1973, Major Taing Chhirc was following news closely from Edinburgh. After service in Lon Nol's army, he was now in Scotland studying engineering. Meanwhile, back in Cambodia, a spiritual awakening had begun, and many were turning to Christ. Chhirc, perceptive and courageous, saw the need for these new Christians to be nurtured in their faith. He sensed God's clear call to him from Luke 9:23-24 to return to Cambodia despite the huge dangers. There might, he knew, be little time.

In July 1973, he alerted the UK's Keswick Convention to pray. 'You have had the Gospel for centuries,' he said from the platform. 'Why did you never come and tell us?' His words were unforgettable. Then, leaving his wife and young daughter in safety in Scotland, he flew back to Cambodia alone. He travelled via Singapore to visit the OMF International Headquarters. There he urged Michael Griffiths, OMF General Director, and his senior team, to send help.

The mission was at full stretch. Was it right to commit more resources to a new endeavour? Who would go? Just a few months earlier, two women leprosy nurses in South Thailand had been kidnapped and murdered. Was it irresponsible to place missionaries in mortal danger? These were not easy decisions. It was eventually agreed that only unmarried missionaries should be sent, so no children would be orphaned. It was further agreed that no-one should be *required* to go; there would be a call for volunteers.

Don Cormack was in Taiwan at the time, studying Chinese. He was one of five OMF volunteers to enter Cambodia. Joining the others in Phnom Penh in October 1974, he had only a few months before the whole team had to leave again. The country fell to the Khmer Rouge in April 1975. Major Chhirc was martyred soon afterwards.[1]

---

1. It was Chhirc, together with Son Sonne, another significant leader who would also die that year, who travelled to Switzerland in July 1974, to represent the Cambodian church at the historic Lausanne Congress on World Evangelization.

'SHARING IN CHRIST'S SUFFERINGS'

Cambodian Christians learned more of what it means to share in Christ's sufferings than most of us will ever know. And they had a deeper grasp of Christ in them, 'the hope of glory'. They were more than conquerors; and nothing could separate them from the love of God. The story of their church, which, some fifty years after its founding, faced its own Neronian persecution, is a powerful modern-day commentary on the great New Testament themes of suffering and glory.

In the Preface to *Killing Fields, Living Fields*, Don sets out four reasons for writing the book. Listen to the second:

> 'If Cambodian Christians today are aware of the faithfulness, the endurance, and the martyrdom of their spiritual mothers and fathers, I trust this will help keep them from playing fast and loose with the precious and eternal gospel which they have received intact; and which they are now called upon to live out, and pass on to others amid many of the same kinds of testing.'

The Reformation martyrs gave their lives for Christians in the West to receive that precious and eternal gospel 'intact'. But today's western church reflects a casual disregard both for doctrine and for biblical ethics — and we all too easily play fast and loose with the truth we have received. Is this another

God-given opportunity to take stock of ourselves? Will we recognize it? Cambodia's church history has given us an eloquent, costly, and persuasive

WE ALL TOO EASILY PLAY FAST AND LOOSE WITH THE TRUTH WE HAVE RECEIVED

apologetic for 'guarding the gospel'. And this is not only for the church in the West, for surely it applies to the body of Christ right around the world.

Killing Fields, Living Fields is modern history, biography, missiology, church history, political analysis, and good English literature. It is the story of a church first planted in the early twentieth century, growing amid all the cross-currents of south-east Asian politics and economics. It is also a story of God's providence. Parts are harrowing to read, and you may read much of it, as I did, with tears. These excerpts from it show that the transcendent presence of the living God is never withdrawn.

The most insistent question of the human heart in every age and culture is surely this: 'Where is God in suffering?' I believe the story of the Cambodian church shows the true answer to that question, and the only answer worth hearing for the troubled soul or the searching mind. It is simply this. 'God is *right there*, closer than the breath we breathe.

We read in Isaiah that in all the Israelites' affliction, God, too was afflicted; and in Peter's pastoral epistle

that 'the God of all grace, who called you to his
eternal glory in Christ, after you have suffered a little
while, will himself restore you, and make you strong,
firm and steadfast.' Our God, Emmanuel, is with us. He
himself will tend to us. What an intimate picture of
God, and how clearly we see it shown in these stories.
He brings comfort, and heals the broken-hearted;
more, he brings hope, and will, we are promised,
'wipe away every tear from their eyes'.[2]

COMRADE DUCH

In May 1999, the *Far Eastern Economic Review* carried
an article on a man called Kaing Guek Eav, more
commonly known as Comrade Duch.[3] His shocking
story was then picked up by newspapers around the
world. Duch was the Khmer Rouge 'Grand Inquisitor'
and chief executioner, responsible for the torture
and deaths of many thousands of Cambodians. He
had his headquarters in the Tuol Sleng death camp
S21, a former Phnom Penh secondary school. Here he
painstakingly recorded all the 'confessions' made by
his victims, and the cruel tortures inflicted on them.
Following the Vietnamese invasion, and the flight of
the Khmer Rouge from Phnom Penh in January 1979,
he had lain low in the refugee camps, and then in the
countryside along the Thai-Cambodian border. When
discovered by the journalists, he was working as a
maths teacher, his former profession up to the time

---

2. Isaiah 63:9; 1 Peter 5:10; Isaiah 7:14; Psalm 147:3; Revelation 21:4
3. *pron.* Doik

he joined the Khmer Rouge in 1967. Aware that any public statement could lay him open to arrest and trial, he was now meeting with high profile journalists. What he said was unexpected and stunning. He had become a Christian!

Duch told the reporters that in 1993 he had begun to examine world religions. 'I wanted to know everything about Islam, Buddhism and Christianity,' he said. 'After my experience in life, I decided I must give my spirit to God.' From the New Testament Duch learned

'MY BIOGRAPHY IS SOMETHING LIKE PAUL'S'

of the Apostle Paul, who described himself as 'the chief of sinners', and he reflected, 'My biography is something like Paul's.'

Duch's wife had been murdered by a bandit in 1995. Incognito, he was being supported by a fellow Cambodian who was working with an American Christian organization. In January 1996 Duch was baptized in the Battambang River. After the article was published in 1999 (See *Far Eastern Economic Review* 6 May and 13 May), he was arrested and placed in solitary confinement for eleven years, until his eventual trial in 2010 for crimes against humanity. He was sentenced to life in prison, where he died in 2020. Duch would have loved hearing of the Khmer Rouge soldier in Story 9. He is another whom the Lord's 'everlasting arms' enfolded; living proof of God's unconditional mercy and grace.

God is there, longing to forgive all those who are penitent, even men like Comrade Duch, who have committed the worst imaginable genocide. What a gospel!

Julia E M Cameron
Foreword to the First Edition
Updated February 2024

Julia Cameron led communications and publishing endeavours for three global missions. She lives in Oxford where she now runs Dictum Press, *a small independent publishing initiative, and is Honorary Director of Publishing for EFAC**

*Evangelical Fellowship in the Anglican Communion

... Cambodia has achieved a distinction which has so
far eluded even those countries unfortunate enough to
experience the full weight of terror brought to bear by the
most monstrous tyrants of our time; it is the first country to
be transformed into a concentration camp in its entirety. ...
in Cambodia, ignored by the outside world, the unburied
dead cry for vengeance, and the living dead for pity; and cry,
both, in vain.
Bernard Levin, *The Times*, **22 April, 1976**

FEBRUARY - APRIL 1975

THE FLIGHT FROM
PHNOM PENH

THE ANGEL ARMIES OF THE SKY
LOOK DOWN WITH SAD AND WONDERING EYES
TO SEE THE APPROACHING SACRIFICE [6]

Major Taing Chhirc was the Cambodian church's most dynamic and visionary leader, clearly raised up 'for such a time as this.' He had a gentle spirit, was soft-spoken, warm, and humble by nature. Yet beneath that exterior, beat a heart of intense, holy passion for the Kingdom of God in the kingdom of Cambodia.

Years before, not long after he had given his life to Christ, he had stood each day defiantly and silently at the gates of Phnom Penh's city jail where several church pastors had been imprisoned for refusing to stop their gospel ministry. In the summer of 1973, he had spoken compellingly to the Keswick Convention at their annual gathering in the English Lake District, imploring them to pray for the church in Cambodia: 'You have had the gospel for centuries. Why did you take so long to come and share it with us?' No-

---

6. From Henry Milman's Palm Sunday hymn *Ride on, ride on in Majesty*

Major Taing Chhirc

one present in that tent would forget him, or his penetrating question.

Under an overwhelming conviction that God was calling him to leave his studies in Edinburgh and return to Cambodia, Chhirc

NO-ONE PRESENT IN THAT TENT WOULD FORGET HIS PENETRATING QUESTION

headed home, stopping en route in Singapore, to plead with leaders of the Overseas Missionary Fellowship (OMF) to send workers into Cambodia at this crucial hour. With darkness falling and a young church overwhelmed by the hundreds turning to Christ, would OMF join others already there, to minister amid the spiritual hunger and humanitarian crisis? That was his question.

The following year, 1974, saw five of us arriving at Phnom Penh's Pochentong Airport. Chhirc had come personally, to meet each one of us. After barely a few months, the time came when no man, at least no foreign missionary man or woman, could remain any longer without endangering the indigenous church. When the order came, it was terse and uncompromising: 'Everyone out within five days. No exceptions.'

With the beleaguered capital at the point of collapse as the Khmer Rouge noose tightened around it, our names on death-lists, and a warning that there was no hope of rescue if we remained, we prepared to return to the airport for our reluctant exodus. It was 26 February, 1975. Despite knowing that his own death was near, Chhirc came, once more, to a sand-bunker on the runway, now under shelling, to see us safely away on a Red Cross flight to Bangkok. Each with just one small bag in hand, we scrambled aboard. I had grabbed a single copy of every piece of Cambodian Christian literature I could find.

As the engines roared, lifting us circling high above Phnom Penh and safely out of range of gunfire, we found ourselves looking down over the doomed city and the precious ones we were leaving behind. Smoke was visible, rising from various points around its besieged perimeter. A farewell letter from Chhirc was being passed round the cabin. It began, starkly, with words from 2 Kings 2:14: 'Where is the Lord God of Elijah?' As he returned to face his own Gethsemane and death, he was asking us to pray that he and the Cambodian Christian leaders left behind would 'boldly tell our agonizing people about the Lord', and would be given God's blessing and courage to face what lay before them — and 'that God may add many more souls to his young church in Cambodia, and let it grow stronger until the day of his return.'[7]

I thought to myself, if Chhirc pictured us in his mind's eye, taking off in that ancient Dakota, as akin to Elijah

---

7. This letter, dated 26 February 1975, together with letters which reached us dated 12 March and 4 April, appear in full in *Killing Fields, Living Fields* Chapter 7.

soaring away to glory, then clearly, at this point, his analogy broke down. We were in tears. We were riven with deep feelings of bereavement, guilt and despair. But I had no doubt that our beloved Chhirc was

WE WERE RIVEN WITH FEELINGS OF BEREAVEMENT

blessed with a double portion of God's spirit as he returned to face the lion's mouth.

At this point, we could never have imagined how indescribably brutal the situation was about to become. That was not clear for several weeks till baleful reports, brought by fleeing refugees at the Thai border, began to hit the headlines around the world. This news only compounded the pain in our hearts.

Leaving benighted Phnom Penh and finding myself — within an hour or so — in the noisy glare and ephemeral, disinterested world of Bangkok, was a shock. Where, in my heart, did I belong? – an Englishman with Canadian citizenship, not three years into my first missionary term, first diverted to Chefoo School, Malaysia, then called away from Taiwan to Cambodia, and, having tackled four Asian languages, now washed up in Bangkok with an uncertain future... I believe there is an identity crisis which every missionary sooner or later must face. For unless our sense of identity, belonging and citizenship is rooted in the Kingdom of God, and our vocation one of self-forgetful discipleship and service to Christ and his gospel, we shall be driven to despair. We are called by God to be his holy people, a counter-culture shaped not by the world but by Christ, wherever he calls us.

We sat in the OMF mission home in Bangkok listening anxiously to every news broadcast, pouring over the newspapers, and earnestly praying for those we had left behind. On the day after Cambodia fell to the Khmer Rouge, wanting to be close, I travelled out to Aranyaprathet on the Thai/Cambodian border,

CITIZENS OF THE TOWN WERE WISTFULLY GAZING ACROSS AT US

and watched as black-clad Khmer Rouge soldiers stretched rolled barbed-wire across the wooden bridge into Poipet, closing it on the Cambodian side. Behind them, citizens of the town were wistfully gazing back across at us. Did they have any idea of the terror about to befall them?

A few more letters were brought out by teams of exhausted, evacuating medics. Then on Good Friday, crucifixion day, we received a final note from Chhirc. It said, simply and poignantly: 'For me to live is Christ and to die is gain.' The word 'die' had been underscored three times. ♦

THE FALL OF
PHNOM PENH

On Thursday 17 April 1975, Cambodia fell to the Khmer Rouge. For a while people were beguiled into thinking this was time for celebration. But as the narrative unfolded, more cruelty was inflicted on that one single nation than the human mind can imagine. Cambodia was turned into the 'Killing Fields'.

During the fearful night of 16th April, the enemy hordes who had been laying siege for the past four months made their final lunge at the city's trembling heart. The thrust was accompanied by a constant and terrifying barrage of rockets and shells fired at will into the defenceless city which now lay utterly helpless. First, Pochentong airport, and then the defence line to the north of the city collapsed. Thousands of weary and discouraged foot soldiers, along with hordes of terrified people from the outskirts, began streaming into the central streets of the shrinking enclave, wandering about, confused and aimless, looking for food and shelter. With the first blush of dawn in the eastern sky across the Mekong River, on the morning of 17th April, there could be seen a deep red glow from fires burning

THE ENEMY HORDES MADE THEIR FINAL LUNGE AT THE CITY'S TREMBLING HEART

to the north and south. Huge clouds of dark smoke ascended from burning fuel depots and from the acres of crowded ramshackle refugee slum dwellings which clung pitifully all around the beleaguered capital.

As the merciless April sun crept higher into a cloudless sky on that never-to-be-forgotten day, the sleepless and benumbed millions of Phnom Penh's people were greeted by the almost festive sight of hundreds of white flags and banners fluttering from every conceivable place: windows, roof-tops, vehicles, and from gunboats steaming up and down the river in front of the Palace. The Khmer Republic had surrendered. Phnom Penh had fallen. All that remained now was for it to be dismembered and thrown like refuse to the four winds.

By 8.00am the atmosphere on the city streets was no longer one of doom but of euphoria. The war was finally over, and the enormous sense of relief that surrender brings was seen everywhere in the crowds of cheering, hand-clapping children, students and flower-throwing women. Many were out in the streets joining in the festivities, dancing and embracing, both civilians and former soldiers. All along the tree-lined boulevards through the centre of the city, the revellers rejoiced that peace had finally come. Enthusiastically, they greeted the columns of bemused and sober-looking Khmer Rouge soldiers clad uniformly in their notorious black pyjama-like fatigues, walking, or riding in armoured vehicles all along the central Monivong Boulevard. Thousands of elated voices were crying, 'Peace, peace!' and leaping for joy, venting months of pent-up emotional anxiety in wild abandon. It was all over: five tumultuous years of cruel civil war, and more than half a million

ELATED VOICES WERE CRYING, 'PEACE, PEACE!' AND LEAPING FOR JOY

Cambodians dead. Yes, the longed-for peace had come at last, they thought.

These tough, battle-hardened young zealots walking through their midst were not monsters after all, but fellow Cambodians, fellow Buddhists, the citizens of Phnom Penh assured themselves. Others, however, hiding behind closed doors, or fearfully peering down from upstairs windows, were more cautious. Theirs was an uncomfortable sense of foreboding. The older ones were perhaps recalling, somewhat cynically, a similar outbreak of ardour five years earlier in 1970, and the heady days immediately following the overthrow of Prince Sihanouk, the advent of the glorious Khmer Republic, Lon Nol, and the promise of massive American support. Five years earlier still, in 1965, crowds had also poured into the streets to join in anti-American demonstrations, and the new spirit of nationalism inspired by Prince Sihanouk, their 'father' prince. The masses are notoriously gullible and fickle, observed some that morning, harbouring distinct feelings of *déjà vu* and more than a little apprehensive at the bizarre spectacle of this victory parade of communist Chinese-backed Khmer guerrillas, and talk of the return of Prince Sihanouk as their head.

Then, quite suddenly, it happened. At 9.30am, as if according to some pre-arranged cue, the patriotic martial music which had been playing non-stop for several days over the radio was switched off. There followed a pregnant pause. And then a voice, harsh and strident:

> Long live the glorious powerful and ever victorious revolutionary forces of Cambodia; long live the great and valiant Cambodian people. We have not come to negotiate but are entering the capital by force!

At 10.00am the Buddhist Patriarch's voice was broadcast, calling for order: 'The war is over, we are among brothers. Stay quietly in your homes,' he said reassuringly. (Within months the top Buddhist clergy would be murdered, temples desecrated and destroyed, and Buddhist idols and relics smashed. During this regime of 'Buddhist brothers', between 40-60,000 monks would be killed.)

Having taken over the radio station and the Ministry of Information, the Khmer Rouge began requesting all former political leaders to meet at the Information Ministry 'to discuss ways of restoring order to the capital'. This was the first in a series of brilliantly-orchestrated lies which the Khmer Rouge set in motion to secure their hold on a people psychologically ready to eat out of their hands. In the ensuing days, thousands of relieved and ambitious military officers and other high-ranking political figures from all over the country, would be 'chauffeured' to their deaths, many proudly

THOUSANDS OF MILITARY OFFICERS WOULD BE 'CHAUFFEURED' TO THEIR DEATHS

wearing their medals and military finery — some even carrying expensive gifts for their beloved Prince/King Sihanouk who would 'receive them as heroes'. The magnetic and backscratching names of Sihanouk and Buddhism were regularly invoked by the wily Khmer Rouge propagandists to cajole, manipulate, and dupe the war-weary masses of unsuspecting Cambodians. These were just the first to be entrapped and brutally slaughtered in cleverly-spun invisible webs of deceit.

That morning about fifty former Republican leaders surrendered themselves at the Ministry of Information. They included the loyal Prime Minister Long Boret, looking nervous and totally exhausted from long torturous days and sleepless nights, struggling with unresolvable political problems, and untold personal agonies. Long Boret and other prominent leaders were all immediately executed at the Phnom Penh Sporting Club, near Wat Phnom: beheaded on the tennis courts. Some say the Khmer Rouge washed their feet in the blood.[4]

In Peking meanwhile, at his headquarters, a jubilant Prince Sihanouk, puppet head of the Khmer Rouge, was fêting the victory at a cocktail party, declaring it 'the finest page in Cambodia's history!' A few days later, in exile in Peking, his mother, Queen Sisowath Kossamak died, adding an appropriate note of irony. It was the end of an era.

As the sun blazed across the sky, the mood on the streets of Phnom Penh was rapidly turning sour. The hand-clapping and dancing gave way to the sound of gunshots and bull-horns. 'Everyone out! Out! Out!' the Khmer Rouge were screaming. The entire population, including about 10,000 Christians, was being compelled at gunpoint to leave the city immediately and head into the parched, war-torn countryside, under the scorching April sun, for 're-education'. Now hundreds of menacing, grim-faced Khmer Rouge, guns at the ready, were striding up and down the streets, moving systematically from door to door all over the city, ordering the numbed and terror-stricken occupants to get out at once. Any who reasoned, argued, procrastinated, or simply got in the way, were summarily shot down in a burst of bullets, a

---

4. Taing Chhirc (See *Killing Fields, Living Fields* Chapter 8) is believed to have been among them.

sobering example to others. Pol Pot's instant agrarian, communist utopia was about to begin. It was 'Year Zero'.

Wholesale looting was also getting underway by the mostly teenage soldiers of the Khmer Rouge who had always boasted that they never stole so much as 'a grain of rice' from the people. They were now confiscating at gunpoint anything they desired, from watches to motorcycles. It was at this time that the people began hearing with increasing regularity, sinister words on the lips of the Khmer Rouge: *Angka* Loeu (the Organization on High). Whatever soulless, faceless, Orwellian monster *Angka* Loeu was, clearly it was the ultimate authority, the new name in which all things were to be done.

By mid-afternoon on that apocalyptic day, the streets were filled with the awesome spectacle of a great forced exodus of between two and three million terrified people being herded like cattle, out into the waterless and war-torn countryside in the searing heat of mid-April. The order to leave was absolute, and without exception: the old and frail, pregnant women, tiny children, malnourished little orphans, the sick and dying, and the hundreds of seriously-wounded war victims still on their beds; thrown out like garbage into the gutter,

MANY GRAVELY ILL, AND BARELY ABLE TO CRAWL, WERE PUSHED OUT ONTO THE STREETS

and told to move on. An estimated 20,000 hospital patients, many gravely ill and barely able to crawl, were pushed out onto the streets that 'victory day'. This was the most pitiful sight of all, as hundreds of them lay helpless, where they had been tipped out into the city's hospital compounds.

The late Sidney Schanberg, a reporter with the *New York Times*, who had stayed to witness the fall of the city, movingly described the scene unfolding before his eyes:

> Two million people in stunned silence — walking, cycling, pushing cars, covering the roads like a human carpet — suddenly forced to abandon the capital... bent under sacks of belongings hastily thrown together when the heavily armed soldiers came and asked them to leave immediately... hospital patients hovering between life and death dragged out of the city in their beds, some with the saline drips still fixed in their arms.[5]

This same wretched drama would be staged in every city and town throughout the entire country. The script of the tragedy had long been written, polished, and rehearsed deep in the dark and inscrutable pre-meditations of 'The Organization'. But it was here in Phnom Penh, on 17 April, 1975 that the heartless

5. I am indebted to Sidney Schanberg for his award-winning, graphic eye-witness dispatches from Phnom Penh, describing the events of this fateful day in Cambodia's history. (*New York Times*, May 1975.)

young zealots of the People's Liberation Army, like a thousand busy and uniformed stage hands, managed the opening matinée. ◆

TEN STORIES
1975-1979

1. VAN REAN'S STORY

On Christmas Day 1977 a group of Christians in the border camp of Aranyaprathet put on a nativity play. It was to change the life of one middle-aged, educated gentleman who had miraculously escaped slaughter at the hands of the Khmer Rouge.

The impact on the camp of that nativity play was enormous. Right after the Christmas Day celebrations, a tall middle-aged Cambodian man came over and handed me a sealed envelope. Inside, a very serious letter in formal Cambodian written style had been drafted. Attached to it was an ID-sized photograph of the gentleman, and beneath the final greeting was his thumbprint:

Aranyaprathet Refugee Camp
25 December, 1977

Kindly allow me to enter and embrace the Christian faith from 1 January, 1978 onwards. I can see without a shadow of doubt that the way of Jesus Christ is the way of salvation, the means of rescuing all mankind. With my highest respect I hereby affirm this with the thumbprint of my right hand.

Mr Van Rean became a devoted disciple of Christ, and a much loved 'uncle' to many in the church. A few months earlier, we had heard through the resistance grapevine in the camp that they had helped Mr Van Rean, a prime target of the Khmer Rouge pogroms, to escape from his commune at a place called 'The Eyes of God'. He was kept hidden somewhere deep in the forest, and was very weak and in rags. The Christians immediately sent in food, clothing, medicines and a mosquito net with one of the resistance couriers, and his life was saved. Shortly afterwards he entered the camp and saw the Christmas play. But the seed which was now bearing fruit was the Word of God sown many years before. Van Rean recalled how 25 years earlier in 1953, he had been given the Book of Proverbs. The wisdom of that book had thrilled his soul and left him forever thirsty for more.

Eventually he was resettled in the USA. Unlike many, he resisted the temptation to re-marry in the camp and prayed patiently for his wife and family still in Cambodia. Much later, I heard that all the family had escaped and were reunited with this dear brother in America. For Van Rean, his unique thumbprint was the only appropriate way to seal the written covenant he made with his Redeemer that Christmas Day in 1977. ◆

2. CHEN'S STORY

*'How beautiful are the feet of those who
bring good news'*

This teenager, with everything stacked against him,
had found a cause to live for. It throbbed through
his weak body. He would use whatever life was left in
him to tell others about it.

Chen was 14 years old and had been brought from
the border to the Khao I Dang camp hospital because
he was terminally ill with stomach cancer. With him
was his elder brother Chem who was 16. Both were
country lads and came from a small village about
40 kilometres inside Cambodia. They were from a
Buddhist family but had become Christians, and most
days I used to sit with Chen in the hospital. We would
read Bible stories together and discuss their meaning.

One day he took me completely off guard when he
said, 'Uncle, in my village, back in Cambodia, no one
has ever heard the gospel of Jesus Christ. I want you
to go and tell them.' Not very convincingly, I tried to
explain that the country was closed to foreigners,
it was illegal, and the mission I worked with would
never allow it. He was puzzled that these human
constraints should stand in the way of taking the
Christian gospel to those who desperately needed it.

I suggested we pray that God would send a Cambodian Christian to his village.

HE WAS PUZZLED THAT THESE HUMAN CONSTRAINTS SHOULD STAND IN THE WAY

A few days later, he greeted me with his usual sunny smile and proceeded to explain that since I wouldn't go, and no-one else was able to go, he would go himself. 'But you are so weak and thin,' I reminded him. 'You need to remain here where you can be cared for properly.' Nothing however would alter his mind. 'Chem has agreed to come with me and help me,' he said. His mind was made up.

The doctors had operated on Chen some weeks earlier, but it was too late. They had given him about three months to live. Armed with tracts and gospels, he returned with Chem to the border, and then set off back to his village. Not only did Chen have advanced cancer, but the way was fraught with dangers: mines, bandits, Khmer Rouge guerrillas, and all the privations of war-torn post 'Killing Fields' Cambodia. He was probably about the 'weakest', most 'foolish', 'lowly' and 'despised' Christian to be found anywhere in the border refugee settlements at that time. But he was the one who gladly trusted and obeyed when the Lord beckoned.

'BEHOLD YOUR GOD. HE COMES TO YOU HUMBLE'

'Behold your God. He comes to you humble'. One can

Little Chen's cross woven from the tubing of his saline drip,
which he gave me shortly before he died.

hardly imagine the amazement of those Cambodian
villagers when this pathetic-looking little lad, leaning
on two crutches, stood before them holding out

41

his gospel tracts. Most of them would have given all they had to have been in the place he had just left, a secure refugee camp complete with food and medicines and a possible sponsorship to America. What important message was this that had compelled him to return so willingly to them? Chen explained later how some in the village received him gladly, while others were disdainful. But only eternity will disclose the consequences of Chen's unique mission to that village.

He died soon afterwards, on the Cambodian border. His ashes are interred at Christ Church in Bangkok. Now he is free from his pain, though he never complained. He is safe 'at home with the Lord'. But I have one unforgettable memory of Chen. It is the appearance of his feet. His little feet were skin and bone, caked with grime, battered and bruised. Yet in all my life will I ever see a more beautiful pair of feet than those? They were so swift to go with the glad tidings of salvation. Chen, in the sheer beauty and simplicity of his faith, saw an urgent spiritual need, realised that he was the one being called to fulfil it, and went straightaway and did it. And I still have the little cross which he wove for me from the plastic tubing of his saline drip. Chen had a way of making something beautiful out of something painful. ♦

3. EVENTS ON THE THIRD ANNIVERSARY

The Lord clearly had his hand on a seemingly-random lining up of young men and women. Radha would fulfil a role in ministry, decades on, which could never have been imagined.

The third anniversary of the fall of Phnom Penh on 17 April, 1978, was marked in a special way with 'weddings'. Young Radha, who was a Christian, feared he would be forced to marry someone who did not share his faith. It was a very tense day.

On the anniversary of 'the glorious revolution', local mouthpieces of *Angka* decreed certain young men and women were to marry in a mass 'revolutionary' ceremony. *Angka* needed more lives, it appeared. Nineteen couples were selected. For Radha it was yet another blow. How could he, a Christian, marry an unbeliever, and someone he didn't even know. Yes, he did long for a Christian wife and a family of his own, especially now, to love and cherish, but not this insane experiment in revolutionary social engineering. Where on earth was God in all this, he thought gloomily. To *Angka* he was deemed good breeding stock to be used to produce children for the revolution, children whom *Angka* would then take away and raise in its own grotesque image.

Mass pairing ceremonies such as this took place throughout the land, usually coinciding with the 'celebrations' surrounding the anniversary of 'the great day of liberation' on 17 April 1975. The couples, complete strangers to each other, would be given a few days together to consummate the 'marriage', sometimes even under the leering eyes of *Angka*'s lackeys, especially if a couple were suspected of being less than enthusiastic about *Angka*'s revolutionary form of nuptial bliss. Following this, the couples would be separated for months at a time as each returned to their male and female mobile work brigades and separate dormitories. As with religion, so with marriage; the family as traditionally understood was abolished in *Angka*'s 'brave new world'.

On the appointed day, Radha hardly dared raise his eyes to look at the mysterious young girl sitting opposite him in the line of women. She too had her head lowered. Neither did he pay any heed to the usual barrage of inane political propaganda, and exhortations to 'join together and build a glorious new Cambodia under the inspired leadership of *Angka*'. He could only see before his eyes and hear ringing in his ears the familiar words from the New Testament, written to the church in Corinth, urging Christians not to marry unbelievers. He felt utterly trapped and helpless. Three times already, he had refused to marry *Angka*'s chosen partner. To refuse again would be his death.

The ceremony over, the nineteen couples, in gloomy silence, were led to their dismal quarters. They were to form the nucleus of a new model village, and to live here together for one month. His new wife had with her a younger sister, and she was permitted to stay with them. On arriving at their appointed home, the sister baked a

NINETEEN COUPLES, IN GLOOMY SILENCE, WERE LED TO THEIR DISMAL QUARTERS

few cakes with some flour which the Khmer Rouge had graciously provided for the occasion, and laid them before the young couple who as yet had barely even spoken to each other. Radha, without thinking, 'carelessly' bowed his head and whispered: 'Thank you Lord for this food.' At once the young woman in front of him stiffened and cried out, 'You are a Christian!' Radha's throat went dry and his heart raced. How foolish he had been! Was she a quisling? Would this be reported? Anxiously, he looked up at the woman, but her face was radiant, and for the first time he perceived in her a deep inner beauty, and a loveliness which even her regulation black clothing could not conceal. Leaning over towards him she confided, 'I too am a

WAS SHE A QUISLING? WOULD THIS BE REPORTED?

Christian just like you, husband!' Her face was glowing with joy. Excitedly they spoke of the past, their home churches in Phnom Penh, friends and mutual acquaintances. She was none other than the charming and winsome daughter of Pastor Choy.

Both were overcome by the goodness and overruling hand of God, and the miracle of their being brought together in such a way. Radha had found all he ever wanted, more than filling the void left in his life by the deaths of his father and six brothers and sisters. Now he had his own family, and his bereaved mother had a new and devoted daughter. They lived quietly and happily together through those final chaotic months of *Angka*'s reign of terror. With the coming of the Vietnamese, they would be swept up in a great flood of refugees moving westward towards Thailand and beyond into all the world. ♦

Radha and his wife settled in the US in the 1980s with their family, including a few who had been separated from them in the Khmer Rouge years. His life has been given to pastoring and teaching in Cambodian churches which have sprung up all across the United States amongst Cambodian diaspora. He constantly travels back to Cambodia with Cambodia Ministries for Christ International, an organization he leads, dedicated to evangelism, church-planting, teaching, and translating Christian books and materials into Cambodian.

4. PASTOR REACH YEAH'S STORY

While many of Cambodia's mighty men and women of faith perished seemingly ignominiously during these four terrible years, some, in God's providence, were miraculously preserved. 'Hidden' would best describe it. Reach Yeah, the last elected national church president, was a perfect example of one of these.

During 1976, as food became more and more scarce and many people around him began to die of starvation and sickness, Yeah and his family were moved to another place further over in Kratie province.

On arriving here, Yeah suddenly feared for his life. Sitting among the Khmer Rouge cadres was a familiar face. The man's name was Pon. Pastor Yeah had known him well in Phnom Penh, but had no idea that he was a Khmer Rouge. Like many Khmer Rouge and their sympathisers, Pon lived an outwardly normal life in Phnom Penh, but he was actually a spy. Knowing how the communists hated Christianity, Yeah, a pastor, and indeed the President of the Cambodian Evangelical

PON LIVED AN OUTWARDLY NORMAL LIFE, BUT WAS ACTUALLY A SPY

Church, felt very vulnerable. He never dreamed that he would meet someone way out here in the northern wilderness regions of Cambodia who would know so completely who he really was. It would only be a matter of time before he was accused and taken away to certain death.

Yeah began to pray earnestly for Comrade Pon, that he might find favour and not hostility in his eyes. To Yeah's great joy, the Lord caused Pon to become unusually friendly towards him, displaying genuine respect for Yeah's age and wisdom. Furthermore, Pon frequently took Yeah aside to question him about his faith in God, clearly not with any malicious motive, but with a deep inner thirst for spiritual truth. Yeah, with long experience, shrewdness, and profound understanding of the ways of Cambodian Buddhist hearts, gently witnessed to this Khmer Rouge cadre of the Saviour Jesus Christ. It seemed to Yeah much of the time that he had his head 'in the lion's mouth', for who could tell what changing circumstance or whim of temper might at any moment turn this thoughtful comrade into his killer.

In time, Yeah felt confident and bold enough to show Pon his hidden Bible, a book strictly forbidden by *Angka*. Now, more fully, he could explain concerning the Creator-Redeemer God and his great design centred on Jesus Christ, the Son. On one occasion when they were discussing communist revolutionary philosophy, and the ideas propounded by the

'Organization', Yeah handed his Bible to Pon opened at Acts 4:32-35. He explained how the first Christians were 'one in heart and mind,' with no one claiming anything as exclusively his own, but rather, as stewards, they held what they had received from God with open hands, gladly and voluntarily sharing all things in common, with the result that there was not a needy person among them. The young cadre was amazed. 'You see,' said Yeah, smiling, 'I have been a radical too, for nearly thirty years, ever since I became a disciple of the Lord Jesus at the age of eighteen.' 'Truly,' beamed Pon, 'you, Grandfather, have trodden the revolutionary way far longer and deeper than any of us!'

Such were the opportunities granted to this wise old 'revolutionary', who with Bible in hand, shrewd as a serpent, innocent as a dove, bore witness to Pon and a good many more of *Angka*'s revolutionaries. But Yeah was always careful to speak only when asked. Otherwise he held his peace.

For the remainder of the Khmer Rouge period, until early 1979, Reach Yeah and family lived hedged around by God's restraining hand, provided for, and content. Thus while others laboured and died in the fields, he was given the responsibility of caring for God's humbler creatures, the cows and buffaloes. Each day he continued to lead them out to graze in some quiet place near the tranquil and majestic forest. There, too, in the midst of God's creation, Yeah kept a divine appointment.

Yeah's Christian faith and love had long been affirmed and nurtured by the fact that God was the Creator. The tangible beauty and vast variety of his handiwork abundantly confirmed that all around him. I recall how, soon after arriving in Cambodia in 1974, we were advised by Yeah:

> 'In your proclamation of the gospel here, you must begin by telling our people about God as Creator. Begin at Genesis 1:1, "In the beginning God created the heaven and the earth…".'

Now Yeah himself was being sustained and renewed as he, an image-bearing creature of the Creator, dwelt there in the quiet pastoral solitude of the Lord's appointment, in the company of grazing cattle.

It was here that it dawned on Yeah, as he ruminated over Scriptures he had memorized for years, that his testimony was exactly that of David, in Psalm 23. He was being shepherded in these green pastures, and lacked nothing. His soul was basking in the warmth and peace of his Lord's immediate presence, even here in a land which had become a dismal valley of shadows where death stalked everywhere. The Khmer Rouge, his 'enemy', was kind to him, and his table was provided with sufficient food.

From time to time, passers-by would surprise Pastor Yeah by inquiring, 'Who is that stranger who comes and goes and sits on the steps of your house?' At first Yeah was puzzled by this, for he was aware of no friend whom he had entertained or who might linger at the door of his house. But as the gossip persisted, Yeah came to understand who the stranger was, even though his own eyes were never opened to see him. Only the villagers and some Khmer Rouge saw him, and soon they too realized and feared. That simple thatch hut, on the edge of the commune, stood on sacred ground. It was visited with angelic protection, and no one dared to violate it. ♦

Christians at the Khao-I-Dang refugee camp church on the Thai-Cambodian border gather in groups to pray for Cambodia.

Young men led away to execution. A painting by a survivor of the Tuol Sleng extermination camp, on display in the genocide museum in Phnom Penh.

Van Rean's covenant made with his Saviour, sealed with his thumbprint made from a paste of soot and ashes.

Meeting Pastor Hom of Battambang and some of his flock who had just made it to the safety of a makeshift encampment on the forested Thai-Cambodian border.

The importunate boy beside his brother in a malaria coma, in a jungle clearing. The saline drip in his arm is hanging from a nearby sapling.

Skulls from the killing fields.

The signpost stands over one of the many mass graves at the Choeung Ek Killing Field where 17,000 people from S.21 Tuol Sleng interrogation/ torture centre were executed. This is just one of thousands of such places all across Cambodia.

The Khmer National Anthem blasted from loud speakers across the fields. This would have been the jarring soundscape to the deaths of Haim and his family.

Bright red blood which covers our fields and plains, of
Kampuchea, our motherland!
Sublime blood of workers and peasants,
Sublime blood of revolutionary men and women fighters!
The blood changing into unrelenting hatred
And resolute struggle,
On April 17th, under the flag of the Revolution, Free from
slavery!

5. HAIM AND HIS FAMILY FACE THEIR EXECUTION

Whole families were often executed together in these fearful years. The way that Haim and his wife and children faced their deaths was whispered about for a long time. The author learned of it from a refugee.

Haim knew that the youthful black-clad Khmer Rouge soldiers now heading across the field were coming this time for him.

Leaning weakly against his hoe for support – itself ironically the primary instrument of execution – he watched their easy, menacing, unhurried pace. He was determined that when his turn came, he would die with dignity and without complaint. Since 'Liberation' on 17 April 1975, what Cambodian had not considered this day?

Haim's entire family was rounded up that afternoon. They were 'the old dandruff', 'bad blood', 'enemies of the revolution', 'CIA agents'. They were Christians.

The family spent a sleepless night comforting one another and praying for each other as they lay bound together in the dewy grass beneath a stand of friendly trees. Next morning the teenage soldiers returned and led them to the nearby *viel somlap*, the 'killing field'.

Curious villagers foraging in the bush nearby lingered, half hidden, watching the familiar routine as the family were ordered to dig a large grave for themselves. Then, consenting to Haim's request for a moment to prepare themselves for death, father, mother and children, hands linked, knelt together around the gaping pit. With loud cries to God, Haim began exhorting both the Khmer Rouge and all those around to repent and believe the gospel.

In panic, one of Haim's young sons suddenly bolted into the scrub. With amazing coolness, Haim prevailed upon the Khmer Rouge to allow him to go and call the boy back.

'What comparison, my son,' he called out, 'stealing a few more days of life as a fugitive in that forest, wretched and alone, to joining your family here momentarily around this grave, but soon around the throne of God, free forever in Paradise?' After a few tense moments, the lad, weeping, walked slowly back to his place with the kneeling family. 'Now we are ready to go,' Haim told the Khmer Rouge.

'NOW WE ARE READY TO GO,' HAIM TOLD THE KHMER ROUGE

By this time not a soldier standing there had the heart to raise his hoe on the backs of these noble heads. Ultimately this had to be done by the Khmer Rouge Chief, who had not witnessed these things. But few of those watching doubted that as each of these Christians' bodies toppled silently into

> *NO SOLDIER HAD THE HEART TO RAISE HIS HOE ON THESE NOBLE HEADS*

the earthen pit which the victims themselves had prepared, their souls soared heavenward to a place prepared by the Lord.

Reports like these were spread widely and not always by Christians, but by typical Cambodians who, until then, had despised the *Puok Yesu.* ♦

6. CHRISTMAS!

'Watchman, what remains of the night? Watchman,
what remains of the night?'
And the watchman replied:
'Dawn will soon be here, but it is still night.'[8]

Rebina's harrowing tale begins back on that baleful day of 17 April, 1975 when he, his wife and four young children were among the multitudes being herded out of Phnom Penh by the Khmer Rouge soldiers.

By the time I met Rebina in 1980, in a jungle camp on the Thai-Cambodian border, he was all alone, a broken man, only just beginning to recover his sanity after years of torment and grief. And yet, he said, there were times when the presence of God was so close. He was a third generation Christian, son of a church elder, and his grandmother was the godly Granny Naey, but he had become separated from them when the Khmer Rouge split them off in another direction.

Early in his flight from Phnom Penh, at one of the frequent checkpoints where the people were being 'liberated' of their valuables, and vehicles and

8. Based on Isaiah 21:11b, 12

'enemies' were being sniffed out for execution, Rebina was spotted and called aside by one of the soldiers scanning the crowds as they passed by. The young Khmer Rouge cadre suddenly softened his voice, and looking straight at the Christian with eyes full of warmth and compassion said, 'I love you, my brother, but from now on you must always say that you are a simple peasant labourer; otherwise you will in time be killed.'

THE YOUNG CADRE SUDDENLY SOFTENED HIS VOICE

Rebina was so startled by this that he could say nothing, but only stand there transfixed, searching the eyes of this gentle stranger whose message and manner bore no resemblance to the uniform he wore or the gun he carried. The curious encounter was rudely interrupted when a tough, battle-hardened Khmer Rouge woman came over and demanded Rebina's motorcycle.

As he and his family walked away, draped in their pathetic bundles of belongings, he stole a glance backwards. Briefly, he caught a glimpse of the upright figure of the young man in black, looking intently after them till the crowds of people came between them. Rebina never forgot this advice. Shortly afterwards he saw many former teachers, doctors, civil servants, soldiers etc, all volunteering 'to return to Phnom Penh and take up their former employment again and assist in the reconstruction of 'Democratic

Kampuchea'. It was a brilliant ploy and many, hoping for respite from the present misery, unwittingly fell into the deadly embrace of the Khmer Rouge and were quickly disposed of. When these lies no longer worked due to bitter experience, the Khmer Rouge devised others. They had an uncanny knack for duplicity, for setting people up for the kill.

The family was eventually sent to a commune at Chamcar Ler, just west of the city of Kampong Cham. Rebina witnessed many terrible things, but it was in 1977 that the situation became critical. The orders coming down from *Angka* now were that all the 'new people' were enemies and must be totally purged. At Chamcar Ler, with the onset of rains in May of that year, the villagers were surprised by the sudden arrival of many thousands of these pitiful 'new people'. For days, men, women and children were trucked in from all directions. The chilling news being whispered down from the local 'old people' was that all these arrivals had been rounded up and brought here to be killed during the slack season after the new rice crop had been planted. (The Khmer Rouge always killed people after they had first worked them almost to death.) Rebina could hardly believe that so many could be systematically liquidated. But on an appointed day it began. Each day, large groups of the new arrivals

EACH DAY, LARGE GROUPS OF THE NEW ARRIVALS WERE TAKEN AWAY

were called up and taken away. None of them ever returned.

Months later, about November time, when the rains had ceased and villagers drove the buffaloes out into the forested countryside to graze, reports began filtering back of this one and that one having come upon mass shallow graves. Where the rains had washed away the sticky red clay, heads, arms and legs could be seen sticking out of the ground. Some of the gruesome remains were still bound and blindfolded, decomposing in the sodden earth. Still incredulous, Rebina was taken secretly by one of the villagers to see for himself. The sight was beyond description. Rebina had seen many terrible things, but he was stunned by this spectre of massive wilful destruction of an entire class of people.

It was during this horrendous time in late 1977 that Rebina received the news that they had taken and killed his wife and one remaining child. He was about ten kilometres away from the village at the time, at

THEY HAD TAKEN AND KILLED HIS WIFE AND CHILD

a work site. There was no warning, no reason, just 'a call from *Angka*'. 'They've killed your wife and now they will kill you. You can't go back there,' a friend warned him.

Rebina fled into the forest, weeping bitterly, wretched with grief and a depth of pain almost beyond

endurance. He threw himself against a tree and cried uncontrollably, beating his fists hard against the rough bark above his head, crying out to God for strength. How long he stayed there with his head pressed against the wood, he couldn't recall. But when he turned aside he found himself surrounded by several doleful-looking oxen. Curious over the commotion, they had left off grazing and come to stand silently about him, looking
on with their sad watery eyes and wet drooling noses. It was as if they understood. And Rebina's heart was arrested by this strange but nonetheless touching company of mourners, God's creatures who had come to stand silently by him in the forest in his moment of grief. But now he had to flee. Somehow he had to reach another commune in secret.
Mercifully, by dawn he had arrived on the steps of a friend's house.

He managed to merge unnoticed into the new commune. One was much like another.
Through the painful months of 1978, Rebina's mind was stayed by dwelling entirely on the past. To think on the present was intolerable. To think on the future, impossible. It became a time of journeying inwards, rethinking, re-evaluating, gaining new understandings of himself and of God.

In late December 1978, distant rumblings were coming from the south

DISTANT RUMBLINGS WERE COMING FROM THE SOUTH EAST

east. Daily, Rebina noticed the Khmer Rouge cadres growing increasingly restless and irritable. Then one day they started disappearing, following the black columns moving westward. To Rebina and his countrymen, whatever it was that loomed over the eastern horizon could never be worse than the present nightmare. Just the prospect of change filled their hearts with fresh hope that perhaps there was life after *Angka*.

A brief and eerie hiatus hung in the air between the silent departure of the last Khmer Rouge and the noisy arrival of the Vietnamese. Momentarily, they were suspended in time, yawing uneasily between two worlds, the one utterly despised, setting in the west; the other nervously anticipated, rising out of the east. And over on the Thai border, Cambodian refugees in camps observed in the sky for a number of days, 'V-shaped' formations of large birds winging their way back into Cambodia. It's a good omen, the exiles nodded one to another.

A BRIEF AND EERIE HIATUS HUNG IN THE AIR

From his hiding place in the forest one afternoon, Rebina observed truckloads of uniformed troops driving up to the village. Abandoning his cover, he raced down to meet them and join in the excitement. A truckload of young Vietnamese soldiers had pulled up. They were unloading some sacks of rice for the people. One of them was waving a portable radio.

Rebina pleaded with the soldier to let him have it for just a few moments.

Excitedly, fiddling with the knobs, Rebina scanned the airwaves for something, for anything: some news, a voice from the outside, a word from beyond this land of the shadow of death. And then he heard it ... rising above the crackle and the static ... the sound of voices singing.

> *Silent Night! Holy Night!*
> *All is calm, All is bright*
> *Round yon virgin mother and Child,*
> *Holy Infant, so tender and mild....*
> *Christ the Saviour is born! Christ the Saviour*
>   *is born!*

Rebina looked up through the tears streaming down his face at the smiling young soldier.

'Christmas?' he inquired. 'Is it really Christmas?'
'Yea, yea, Christmas!' called back the youth, seizing his radio as the truck sped off.

A voice had indeed come to him. From outside his sad and quarrelsome world, a clear and precious Word had been spoken through the static and interference. It was the Word of the eternal and creator God, made flesh, suffering along with Rebina, full of grace and truth. Emmanuel. God with us. It was Christmas. ◆

7. PASTOR HOM, HIS FLOCK, AND HIS PERSONAL GRIEF

It is now mid-January 1979, four years after Cambodia's fall to the Khmer Rouge. Ninety percent of the nation's Christians have already been massacred, or have died of disease, overwork, or malnutrition. The Vietnamese army has overrun Cambodia, driving the Khmer Rouge westwards, into the malaria-infested jungle along the Thai border, with many thousands of their Cambodian captives.

Pastor Hom, one of only three pastors to escape the genocide, hears news that the Vietnamese have just captured Phnom Penh. Violence is rife and nowhere is safe. Famine and malaria are both huge threats to survival. His young assistant, Seng, had collapsed and drowned while bathing in the river, racked with disease and overcome by sheer exhaustion. Now, his darling infant son has a high fever.

All Cambodia, it seemed, was on the move. Days were occupied with foraging for rice in the fields. But as the multitudes were all doing the same, they were forced to go deeper into the countryside where a number were killed by lurking Khmer Rouge, gangs of thieves, or from stepping on landmines.

Nights were even more fearful. At the height of the fighting around Tmar Koul, the Christians, unable to sleep, prayed in groups through the darkest hours, out in the fields where they camped.

Although they were free, all the basic means of life now had to be fought for. Water was a major problem. The fleeing Khmer Rouge had purposely polluted wells and pools by throwing dead bodies into them. But there was little choice other than boiling it if you could, and drinking it anyway. Seeing that the food situation was deteriorating rapidly and the fighting around Tmar Koul was still going on, Pastor Hom decided to move them all to Battambang City. It was every man for himself. By the time his family reached the city, so had tens of thousands of others.

Battambang had already been derelict for nearly four years. But now the masses crowded in, chopping down the trees, pillaging, turning everything upside down. All were reduced to foraging around like pigs in a great filthy pigsty. Every day, like all the others, he grimly searched for food, 'like an old buffalo', he mused, hauling his cart behind him. The Khmer Rouge had killed most of the livestock, pigs, chickens, ducks, cattle etc and meat

HE GRIMLY SEARCHED FOR FOOD, 'LIKE AN OLD BUFFALO'

was almost impossible to find. But he had good reason to be thankful for his deft skill, learned in boyhood, of catching field rats. And for rice, he was forced to search for kernels under people's houses or compete with the rats for it in former granaries.

Hom's wife walked for miles every day to find clean water and haul it back. One by one they all became ill. The children had chronic diarrhoea and scabies and then they caught measles. An epidemic was sweeping the slum city of squatters. Running sores infected their eyes and worms crawled from their festering noses and mouths. His youngest child was at the point of death. The little thing was wasting away. His mouth was a mass of sores, gums receding, unable to take any sustenance.

One night at about nine o'clock, Pastor Hom watched him raise a tiny shrivelled fist and with one finger extended, pointed to his tongue. He hadn't been able to speak for days. Hom took an orange which he had earlier traded for some of his precious rice. He squeezed one or two drops into the child's mouth. His wife, weeping silently, coaxed a few drops of milk from her breast onto a curled leaf and eased them into the child's open mouth. Then, having given all they had, they bowed their heads and Hom committed the little boy into the Lord's keeping, concluding 'though you have granted me this great suffering, my heart has not grown small towards you.

I still love you with all my heart. But it is a heart filled with tears.'

At one in the morning, Hom reached out his hand and felt the child's little body. It was stone cold. In the morning they wrapped him up and laid his remains to rest in a little grave they had dug among the trees. But the father could not forget his baby son. He felt sapped of all energy. He cried out to God to please relieve his grief and give him peace, for his heart was deeply shaken.

It was the ceaseless search for a water supply which brought them wandering one day into a vast encampment along the jungled Thai-Cambodian border where I happened to be working. He chanced to hear some people gossiping about a foreign Christian teacher nearby. Surrounded by other Christians who were walking with him, he hurried over. I was just leaving one of the hot and crowded little huts where I had been teaching, and was walking away surrounded by families seeing me off, and the usual throng of curious onlookers and excited children all eager to help carry any bags or books. As we rounded a clump of bamboo atop a dusty knoll at the head of a muddy water hole, we heard them calling out behind us and excitedly waving their arms. I shall never forget turning round in my tracks and seeing the little procession hurrying towards us in single file along the narrow path on the steep bank surrounding the pool. One face, definitely older, haggard and sunburned, shone out above the others. Full of character, it glowed with an unmistakable light and warmth. I said to myself, 'This can only be the beloved Pastor Hom of Battambang.'

ONE FACE GLOWED WITH AN UNMISTAKABLE LIGHT AND WARMTH

All the Christians, with their families and friends around them, seated themselves on the ground beside the tall bamboo. They wasted no time in discarding their tattered black Khmer Rouge rags for the new clothes we provided, and they soon looked once more like typical Cambodian country folk, only much thinner. Facing them, sitting cross-legged behind a cardboard box full of new Cambodian Bibles and hymnbooks, was Pastor Hom. These precious books he began to distribute among his people, most of whom had lost all their Christian literature. It was now time to worship and thank God for all these blessings. Using the cardboard box as his lectern upon which he had placed his own tattered old Bible, he began exhorting his listeners, taking the opportunity clearly and simply to explain the facts of the gospel to all the curious onlookers. I was walking back to the truck for more literature when the singing began. It was so unusual to hear a chorus of voices singing together in unison in such a grim place as this, that I stopped to watch.

The golden colours of evening washed the sky, and the camp was relatively still. As the growing awareness dawned upon them that, yes, they could sing here without fear of death, their voices grew in volume and ardour. Before long I was unable to see the Christians for the vast crowd which was gathering around them to behold the amazing spectacle. Hearing only the sound of their voices from within the midst of the crowd, I began to concentrate on the words they were now singing with a quality of rapture and conviction I had never heard before, or indeed since. It was an old much-loved hymn translated from the English. The last time I heard it sung was in 1975 at Noah's Church (a ship marooned and abandoned on the banks of the Bassac River in Phnom Penh, used as a church) on the waterfront of besieged Phnom Penh. That was just before they entered the fiery crucible. And now here among the exiles it sounded again:

The love of God,
How rich and pure
How measureless and strong;
It shall for evermore endure
The saints' and angels' song.

And the Lord whispered to me in that moment: 'They came forth from the furnace with no smell of the burning upon them'... no trace of bitterness, no anger, no 'why this?' or 'why that?' But there they were, kneeling in the dust, exhausted and hungry, all having lost at least one family member to the Khmer Rouge,

yet extolling the love of God. They were rich with
the fragrance of the knowledge of him: a fragrance
acquired, no doubt, from walking close to the Son
of God through the flames. And I was convinced that
they would have extolled the strong love of God,
as indeed others had, even to the grave, for with
suffering Job, they could repeat, 'Though he slay
me, yet will I hope in him.'
Little wonder the crowds
were drawn irresistibly to
them that day. They were

> **THE CROWDS
> WERE DRAWN
> IRRESISTIBLY TO
> THE AROMA OF
> CHRIST**

being attracted not to religion, not to a band of
defiant survivors, but to the aroma of Christ, lingering
naturally about these very plain earthen vessels there
in the shade of the bamboo along that war-ravaged
border.

Pastor Hom's name in Cambodian means 'fragrant
aroma'. ♦

8. A BOY WHOSE BROTHER IS DYING

Over the course of 1979, hundreds of thousands of sick and skeletal Cambodian refugees attempted to reach makeshift refugee camps on the Thailand border. Some camps grew to be very large.

Following the ousting of the Khmer Rouge by Vietnamese troops in 1979, chaotic refugee settlements sprang up, full of thousands of desperately sick and starving people who had endured the Khmer Rouge four-year reign of terror. These were unlike the UN-managed camps which had existed further inside Thailand since 1975. Though now under Vietnamese control, their erstwhile Khmer Rouge tormentors were now refugees themselves in the forests.

Many of the refugees were lost, parent-less children. As they came into the forest clearing, each child was bathed, and dressed in clean clothes. Sometimes as you peeled the coarse rancid garments from their scrawny little bodies, with clothes patched, repaired and repatched, close inspection would reveal another world gone forever. Here, an ancient tear painstakingly and resourcefully sewn with such a neat row of little stitches that could only have been done by the caring hands of a mother, a mother desperately trying to prolong the life of the only shirt her little one possessed. And as you fingered those tiny stitches and looked again into the dark, melancholy eyes of the child, it was just possible to recover a fleeting glimpse of that lost world. A mother had borne, loved and protected this child. A Cambodian mother had fought valiantly right here to recover some measure of dignity, some vestige of normal family life, some covering against all the powerful forces arrayed against her and her child. But evil hands had torn and ripped her world to shreds. And all that remained for us to do was drop the filthy rags into the fire.

EVIL HANDS HAD TORN AND RIPPED HER WORLD TO SHREDS

One day, as I stood interpreting for one of the only two doctors at this place, called Klong Wah, where thousands needed immediate attention, a little lad of about eight came up to me calling, 'Uncle, uncle, please come and help me carry my older brother over here where he can be given medicine.'

The boy explained that his brother, about 12, was lying a good two kilometres away in the bush, unconscious in a malaria coma. But I couldn't just walk away from my responsibilities as interpreter and the enormous task I already had on my hands, helping to care for hundreds of dying people right there. I knew that only a few yards into the forest there were more, unseen, who needed help. How could I justify going so far and using up so much valuable time for just one? I told the boy I couldn't go with him, but to get one or two others to help carry his brother in.

Of course I knew even as I spoke that it was unlikely anyone was going to expend their own limited energy on a dying boy. His bad *karma*, his fate, had brought him to this sorry state, they might be reckoning subconsciously. Who can alter *karma*? Certainly the fit and healthy young Khmer Rouge men and women who lounged around in their own exclusive shelters, cooking their pots of rice and remaining aloof from these 'slaves' and 'class enemies' wouldn't lift a finger to help. When once we did try to harness their energies to assist in the washing of the sick, they absconded as soon as our backs were turned, unwilling to get their hands dirty or to risk infection. They even abandoned their own when it looked like a hopeless case.

This boy, however, would not be put off. He persisted in crying out after me, until I finally steeled myself and ignored him. After about an hour of whimpering and pleading, he fell silent, deep in thought. He knew that I was the only lifeline there was to save his brother's life. Next thing, I felt a pair of sinewy arms grip me round the legs, and a pair of ankles lock around mine. And there he clung like a leech. Now it was my turn to protest. But his lips were sealed.

I FELT A PAIR OF ANKLES LOCK AROUND MINE

He clearly wasn't going to let go his vice-like grip on my legs till they followed him to that place where his brother lay dying. I was thus compelled to go with him in order to get rid of him!

His dogged importunity had gained him the victory. And I reflected as I pursued him through the trees that this was surely what serious believing Christian prayer was all about. It entailed a crucial element of 'violence'. It involved patiently holding on to the knees of God, even in the face of apparent silence and lack of movement. The older brother's life was saved.

HIS DOGGED IMPORTUNITY GAINED HIM THE VICTORY

But that was not the end of the story. Watching all these things was a French-educated Khmer Rouge cadre who was rather grudgingly helping us take care of the orphans. He was quite bemused by it all and my 'weakness' in caving in to the will of a mere boy. However, later, the incident paved the way for us to talk about the essence of love. What it is, and where it comes from. As a result of the importunate orphan boy, this cadre's heart was opened, and in time he also came to follow Jesus Christ. What became of the boy and the elder brother he saved, I do not know. God knows. The former Khmer Rouge soldier, however, I did meet again, a few years later, attending a church in Vancouver, Canada. ♦

9. A KHMER ROUGE SOLDIER FINDS FORGIVENESS

By late 1979 many Khmer Rouge footsoldiers, scattered, alone and disheartened, were struggling to stay alive. Could God forgive them for the evil and untold suffering they had inflicted on their countrymen?

Thousands of demoralised Khmer Rouge, and the multitudes of dying wretches they had driven into the forests with them under Vietnamese shelling, were spilling over into Thailand. I was helping as an interpreter for two Christian paramedics among those tens of thousands of diseased and malnourished refugees, collapsed all over the forest floor along the Thai-Cambodian border, south of Aranyaprathet. Most were dying of malnutrition, dysentery and cerebral malaria. Midst all the crises and pressures, and with scores of nameless victims being carried away each day to mass graves and an uncertain eternity, it was difficult to feel any sense of the sovereignty of God in their lives, or indeed mine in this terrible place. It was then as I scurried from one emergency to another that my attention was strangely drawn to a young Khmer Rouge soldier lying in the leaves, close to death. Not that there was anything unusual in that, but from his wide questioning eyes which seemed to follow me everywhere as I moved to and fro in front of him, I knew I had to stop and talk with him.

There was nothing else I could do for him in the circumstances except to hold his head, and soothe his burning temples with a damp cloth. Bending close to his ear, I began to talk to him saying that I had some very important 'good news' to tell him.

As I uttered the Cambodian words for 'good news', it struck a chord of recognition within him and he struggled to tell me in a voice full of urgency of a time during the revolutionary war against the Lon Nol regime when he lay wounded under a tree. A stranger from the nearby village had appeared and told him of the Living Creator God and Saviour

HE SECRETLY TRIED TO DISCOVER MORE OF THIS 'GOOD NEWS'

Jesus Christ. Though he secretly tried to discover more of this 'Good News' he never met anyone who could help him. Then in April 1975, following the fall of Phnom Penh and the forced exodus of all the people into the countryside, he found himself a member of the Khmer Rouge garrison guarding the empty capital. On one of his regular patrols he passed a house which had an unusual signboard fading in the sun on its front fence which again spoke of 'Good News'. Day by day as he passed the empty house, it fascinated him, and he wondered who had lived there, and what was this 'Good News' they had. He felt so close to finding the answer to his quest, but the house, like all the buildings in Phnom Penh, lay empty and silent.

Hardly able to restrain my excitement, I asked exactly where in the city the house with the signboard was situated. It was undoubtedly our Good News Centre, at 10 Pologne Avenue! The place where I had lived prior to my flight from the falling city in 1975. Then I told him that it was I who had lived in that house, and now I would gladly tell him the same 'Good News' we had once proclaimed there, and so I did, as he listened intently. That the sovereign hand of God had been upon us both, bringing us together in this far away, seemingly 'godforsaken' no man's land, a place of war and death, and at such a moment, was awesome beyond comprehension.

I know he found peace with God that hot afternoon because the last audible word which passed his lips was 'Jesus', and then he slipped into a deep coma. The next morning when we arrived early at the camp, it was just in time to see

THE LAST AUDIBLE WORD WHICH PASSED HIS LIPS WAS 'JESUS'

the orderlies carrying his stiff and lifeless body away towards the mass burial pits. I went and sat down quietly for a few moments under the trees, beside the place still marked by the crushed leaves where a brother, whose name I never discovered, had lived briefly and then, without moving, died in Christ.

Though it was a grim and terrible place, surely,
I thought, this is holy ground, for here the sovereign
God had appeared to a seeker of the kingdom and
taken him quickly home. And to me, God had given
the reassurance that despite everything, he was still
in control. Furthermore, it dawned on me at that
moment that the Lord's everlasting arms would reach
and enfold even the Khmer Rouge. And so they did
over the months and years which followed. ♦

10. A MOTHER'S LOVE NEVER CEASES

The now defeated Khmer Rouge have been herding pitiful columns of captives up and down the Thai border for weeks. The Thai authorities have been reluctant to let them in. Finally, in 1979, the pressure is unstoppable, and they break through the border, collapsing in their thousands on the Thai side, in the jungle and scrub. Christian and humanitarian organizations have been waiting to help them, but these organizations are soon overwhelmed. That is the context of this little vignette; it shows how a mother's love is an inviolable bond, whatever life brings.

The abject misery of these unfortunate people, who after four years of struggling to survive under the Khmer Rouge, should end up perishing in such a place and in such a way as this, was beyond comprehension. The sheer inhumanity of it all defied reason. If it had been as a result of famine or some natural disaster, it might have been more tolerable. But it was all so needless. And to make matters worse, in order to continue to help them, we had to tiptoe obsequiously around the same sullen Khmer Rouge cadre, and corrupt calculating Thai army officers, who were responsible for it all in the first place.

Most were dying of a lethal strain of cerebral or falciparum malaria compounded by amoebic dysentery, tuberculosis, and starvation. The humid air was heavy with the stench of disease and death. An eerie silence pervaded the place as no one spoke, no one moved unless compelled, and no one cared or even noticed the needs of a neighbour. Their hearts and minds seemed frozen hard, held in the icy grip of an interminable winter.

THE HUMID AIR WAS HEAVY WITH THE STENCH OF DISEASE AND DEATH

They simply squatted, alone, huddled in groups, smoking rolled leaves to alleviate their aching bellies, or lay prostrate, groaning, coughing painfully, twisting this way and that. Some had several layers of dirty grey-black rags wrapped tightly around them to keep in the body heat. They feared coldness as a harbinger of death.

Very occasionally, one would catch a glimpse of some poignant indication of the human spirit, a reminder that all these filthy ragged bundles of bones were in fact human beings after all. I recall a distraught middle-aged Chinese woman stumbling towards me cradling in her arms the long, emaciated body of her totally wasted teenage son. He must have been taller than she was, but now very light, just skin and bones. The lad was all that remained of her family. She must have been dragging him around from place to place like this for days. But despite those steady loving arms around him, his life was fast ebbing away, running through her fingers like sand. She knew she could hold him no longer. As the woman dropped wearily on one knee, her son's limp body fell back over the other. The scene perfectly resembled a medieval sculpture of the weeping Mary holding the crucified Jesus in her arms — a Cambodian pietà.

Unaware that she was being watched, she laid her son carefully on the ground. Then, with a piece of bark, she painstakingly scraped away at a place under a tree until it was clear of leaves and sticks, a smooth levelled area on the black earth. She then unrolled a new straw mat she had acquired and lifted him tenderly onto it. For some time the mother busied herself making him as comfortable as she could, even scooping out a hole beside him in the earth where she could roll him over to relieve himself. Finally, she sat beside him wiping his cavernous face with the corner of her faded sarong. The youth was a picture of despair. His huge panic-stricken eyes were wide and pleading. They seemed to shout at me, 'For God's sake do something!' But in that forest, there was nothing we could do for him medically.

HIS HUGE PANIC-STRICKEN EYES WERE WIDE AND PLEADING

He was in the final stages of starvation. I could only pray for God's mercy, and that his suffering would soon be over.

The next day he was gone. Almost certainly he died during the night, and the mother, for the last time, lifted her only son in those strong arms and bore him away to bury him. She would never have permitted the team of rough orderlies who hauled away the dead every morning, to toss her son into the common grave. The secret grave site would have been painstakingly dug out and prepared by the aching, loving hands of that mother. I never saw her again; that awesome, noble lady. But for several days, till falling leaves obliterated it, the neat little clearing under the kapok tree, made by a devoted mother as a deathbed for her son, remained a still-life portrait of love.

REFLECTING

AFTERWORD

These stories are just a few of the many I recorded while working among the exiles from Cambodia's 'killing fields', sheltering in refugee prisons and camps along the jungled Thai-Cambodian border after 1975, when I, too, had been forced to flee from Phnom Penh. These were the years when Cambodia was closed off from the outside world, its people enduring a four-year-long reign of terror, followed by a decade of warfare and further communist oppression under the Vietnamese.

Following the signing of the Paris Peace Accords in 1991, the restoration of freedom of religion, and King Sihanouk's welcoming letter to the church, I made my first exploratory return visit to Phnom Penh. I walked the rubbish-strewn streets, searching out familiar places, only to find them in ruins, torn down, occupied by squatters. But most shocking of all, was Tuol Svay Prey High School which I used to visit with Setha my language teacher. The Khmer Rouge had turned it into their principal interrogation/torture 'Centre S21', Tuol Sleng', presided over by *Angka's* (the Organization on High) grand inquisitor: Comrade Duch.

From there, I took the road leading out of Phnom Penh, down the 17km route taken by the thousands of condemned men, women, and little children from

Tuol Sleng to a cruel death in the 'Choeung Ek Killing Field'. Among the flowering jacaranda trees were numerous open mass graves and a 62metre high glass-walled stupa containing thousands of skulls. There too, stood that now infamous, towering solitary old oak tree, 'the killing tree', leaning, bearing the burden of its hideous past when scores of babies were seized from their condemned mothers' arms, to have their heads dashed against its trunk. Nearby, stood another tree from which the Khmer Rouge had hung speakers playing loud music to drown out the cries and screams of the victims. Thousands of tortured, terrified souls, were transported here to be slaughtered on an industrial scale at the order, the stroke of Comrade Duch's pen—'smash them all!' Amid the scraps of bone and clothing, I stooped and picked up a half-buried shirt-button, and I thought of those trembling fingers that had fastened it on that last terrifying day.

By the kindness of Gilbert Appleby

The killing tree, bearing the burden of its hideous past.

In the middle of the Garden of Eden stood the Tree of Life. Nearby, stood the Tree of the Knowledge of Good and Evil. Man chose to eat the fruit of the latter which, in the fulness of time, led to a killing tree – a cross, outside the city wall, also in a place of skulls, called Golgotha. Down that tree of agony and death, the atoning blood of God Incarnate flowed. Jesus entered our suffering and died on a killing tree in a killing field. In so doing and rising from the grave, he took us back to the Tree of Life. He dealt a death blow to death itself. In the New Creation, flowing from the throne of God and the Lamb, forever scarred, will flow a river of life. On its banks, replanted, the lost Tree of Life for the healing of the nations.

And across Cambodia we are witnessing the healing of a nation, once a charnel house but now being restored to life in the spreading branches of the body of Christ. Among those branches is Comrade Duch. (When they came to arrest him, he declared that for some years he had been a baptized disciple of Christ.) All through his trial for genocide and crimes against humanity, unlike all the other Khmer Rouge arch-criminals, he confessed everything and begged for forgiveness for his crimes. He died in prison with his Bible and hymn book beside him. He never wearied of sharing his faith with his jailors.

On either side of Christ had hung two evil-doers. One just wanted to be released to continue his old life here. The other, recognizing Jesus as his Lord and Saviour, wanted release from guilt, and asked Jesus to remember him when he came into his Kingdom. 'Truly, this day you will be with me in Paradise,' Jesus assured him.

All of us, now, confronted by the cross of Christ, line up behind one of these two men: either mocking, despising, and ignoring Christ, wanting to get on with our lives in our own way; or, acknowledging that he is the eternal Son of God, that he died in *our* place, for *our* sins, and choosing to follow him.

You have read of how Mr Van Rean, little Chen, a dying former Khmer Rouge soldier, and so many others including Comrade Duch responded to the living Christ.

I am reminded of Peter's words in 1 Peter 2:24:

'He himself bore our sins in his body on the tree, that we might die to sin and live to righteousness. By his wounds you have been healed.'

Don Cormack.

Don Cormack
Lent 2024

TIMELINE FROM 1973

TIMELINE

1973-4: Major Taing Chhirc (pp 27-34), Cambodia's foremost visionary leader, calls for urgent help for Cambodia, for prayer and people, from the UK Keswick Convention and then from OMF International in Singapore, as so many Cambodians are turning to Christ.

1975: 1 January 1:20 am: Tens of thousands of Khmer Rouge encircle Phnom Penh, launching their final, decisive bombardment of the city's defense perimeter. Scores of young Christians continue to be baptized in the Mekong River, even as fighting reaches the further shore where villages are burning.

Ever more refugees pour into the besieged capital where cats and dogs are being eaten and rice riots are breaking out. Rockets and artillery shells explode in city streets. Hospitals are overflowing with the wounded. Churches are packed, surrounded by those waiting to get in.

March: Stock-piles of Christian literature are distributed, and some of it hidden. Missionaries, listed for death, are informed they *must* leave on final Red Cross evacuation flights within five days. Continued presence will put Cambodian Christians in great danger. Taing Chhirc who personally met each of them on arrival, now tearfully waits with them in a bunker on the runway. The airport is under fire. He sees them safely away, then returns to the beleaguered city, to his own 'Gethsemane' and martyrdom.

4 April Good Friday: All the Cambodian church leaders meet at Taing Chhirc's home. He reads John 13 and they wash one another's feet.

6 April Easter Day: upwards of 5,000 Christians crowd into Phnom Penh's churches, gathering under trees, in open spaces and abandoned buildings.

15 April Bible School students are forced to flee as the Khmer Rouge advance on Takhmau on the edge of Phnom Penh. Church leaders meet at Pastor Reach Yeah's Bethlehem Church. He is elected National Church President. Like most of the churches, Bethlehem remains full of people worshipping, praying, comforting, as the end approaches.

17 April 8.00am: White flags flutter everywhere as Phnom Penh surrenders. The Khmer Rouge parade victoriously down Monivong Boulevard, greeted by cheering crowds thinking the war is over.

9:30 am: The atmosphere abruptly changes. The entire population of two-and-a-half million, (swollen by over a million refugees from the countryside) with near 10,000 Christians, Protestant and Catholic, are ordered at gunpoint to leave the city and head into the parched, war-torn countryside, under the scorching April sun. Pol Pot's instant agrarian, communist utopia is about to begin. It's Year Zero in Pol Pot's 'Democratic Cambodia'.

17 April, 1975 to 7 January, 1979: All the cities and towns across Cambodia have become empty, rubbish-and-corpse-strewn ghost-towns. The highest ranks of society and military are the first to be purged. Then the educated: 50,000 Buddhist monks, Christians and other 'enemies of the people' are liquidated by *Angka* – the Organization on High'. Extermination camps are set up across the nation, with Tuol Sleng, under the ruthlessly efficient Comrade Duch, at the epicentre. The entire nation, all identically dressed in black pyjamas, is one vast labour camp of soulless communes, subsisting on thin rice soup and secretly foraged grubs, rats and scraps. Gentle Cambodia is now a charnel-house where *Angka's* army of teenage grim-reapers daily purge those who step out of line, or fail to meet their random standards of revolutionary purity.

Up to two million perish, including thousands of Christians (see Haim's family story, Chapter 7) and almost all the church leadership. Those who survive are mostly hardy rural folk, familiar with working in the fields and living on very little. Small groups of Christians whisper prayers and hymns together in secret, led now mostly by elderly grannies and aunties.

Cambodia's ousted god-king, Prince Sihanouk, who had fled to Beijing in 1970 to become titular Head of State in exile of the Khmer Rouge, returns in triumph to Phnom Penh. He is horrified at what he sees and soon 'retires', imprisoned in his derelict royal palace with his wife Monineath and two sons: Prince Sihamoni (later crowned King, 2004) and Prince Narindrapong (dies in Paris, 2004), every day fearing for their lives. Five of the fourteen royal children perish during the Pol Pot years as do fourteen grandchildren.

Thousands of devout royalist peasants had joined the Khmer Rouge, following the example of their god-king Sihanouk, and for fear of the horrendous American carpet-bombing of the countryside.

In 1976, a call goes out to Cambodian students studying overseas, to return and help 'rebuild the motherland'. On arrival, they are summarily executed.

Refugees: young men, former students, soldiers and intellectuals, flee in all directions, mostly to Thailand, to UNHCR camps around the Thai/ Cambodian border. In 1977, Van Rean (p35) arrives in the camp at Aranyaprathet on the Thai border. Resettlement to America, Europe and Australia begins.

In 1978, The Khmer Rouge launch raids into Thailand and Vietnam seeking to recreate the great medieval Khmer empire of Angkor. They begin ruthlessly purging their own ranks especially the Eastern Zone suspected of being pro-Vietnamese rather than pro-Chinese, their principal supporter and sustainer. Mao's radical Red Guards are their inspiration.

25 December, 1978: Vietnam trains and arms dissident Khmer Rouge fleeing the purges, and with 120,000 troops launches a sudden and massive invasion of Cambodia. Within two weeks, their military juggernaut sweeps the Khmer Rouge from power. Pol Pot and all the Khmer Rouge leadership flee into former hideouts in the Thai borderlands, from where they begin a 20-year-long guerrilla war against the government in Phnom Penh.

7 January, 1979: The Vietnamese capture Phnom Penh and install former Khmer Rouge commanders: Hun Sen, Heng Samrin and Chia

Sim as leaders of 'The State of Cambodia'. The Vietnamese army stays in Cambodia for ten years till 1989.

Free from the Khmer Rouge terror, the entire nation is suddenly on the move, returning to home-towns and villages, desperately seeking lost loved-ones. Famine and disease stalk the land following the Khmer Rouge's cruel scorched-earth campaign as they retreated.

Small house-churches spring up, but the new regime is still communist and staunchly anti-Christian. Pastor Reach Yeah (p45) and family sail down the Mekong to Phnom Penh on a raft. His church meets secretly in a banana plantation at Takhmau.

June 1979: The many thousands of sick and starving people whom the defeated Khmer Rouge have been herding into the western forests are finally allowed into Thailand. Huge camps are set up, such as Khao I Dang with 125,000 refugees, including Pastor Hom (p65), and little Chen (p37).

South of Aranyaprathet, along the border, at places like Klong Wah, the notoriously malaria-infested jungle is full of thousands more skeletal refugees, collapsed and helpless on the forest floor. With them, but apart, groups of vanquished Khmer Rouge warily look on. Here the author encounters the importunate boy trying to save his brother (p73); the dying Khmer Rouge soldier (p77); the broken Rebina (p57); and that Chinese mother (p81). Survivors are bussed inland to hastily thrown up Sra Kaew Camp where many, too weak to move, drown in a monsoon downpour on the first night. The Thai military round up 40,000 others and transport them north, forcing them back into Cambodia over a steep ravine and across a valley full of mines. The later ones use the dead as stepping stones. At least 3,000 perish.

1990: Christianity is again formally recognized by the government. Plans are put in place for a new translation of the Bible into modern Khmer (Cambodian) from the original languages and referencing the latest scholarship, under the auspices of the United Bible Society.

1991: The Paris Peace Accords are signed in October by all the Cambodian political factions. 22,000 UN peace-keeping soldiers are sent in to prepare for elections in 1993. The Khmer Rouge refuse to co-operate and continue fighting their guerilla campaign.

1993: The remaining refugee camps in Thailand are closed. Over 200,000 Cambodians, like Radha and his family (p41), have been resettled in third countries: mostly the USA, France and Australia. The remainder are repatriated to Cambodia.

1998: Isolated, overthrown and abandoned, Pol Pot dies in his jungle hideout at Anlong Veng, reportedly of a heart attack. He is burned on a bonfire of old planks and tires, as his erstwhile comrades cry, 'Burn, just burn!'

1999-2020: A pitiful remnant of the once mighty Khmer Rouge, 'The Organization on High', self-destruct in an orgy of squabbling, betrayal and internecine killing. A rump of Khmer Rouge cadre, holed up in Pailin, surrender to the government, to await trial for their massive crimes against humanity. The last stubborn survivor, Ta Mok 'the Butcher', is caught and imprisoned. Just one of them stands apart: the notorious Comrade Duch, commander of the infamous S21 extermination centre, who had signed-off on the torture, and forced confessions of over 15,000 men, women and children, overseeing gruesome deaths with 'Smash them all'. In 1995, he had abandoned the Khmer Rouge and become a committed, baptized Christian. He, alone, pleads guilty to all his heinous crimes and begs for forgiveness. Imprisoned for life, he dies in 2020 with his Bible and hymnbook beside him.

2023: 30,000 Christians from across Cambodia gather to praise and worship God in Phnom Penh on the centenary of the Khmer Evangelical Church founded in 1923. The event is opened by Cambodian Prime Minister, and former Khmer

Rouge combatant, Hun Sen, and closed by his son and successor Hun Manet.

There are estimated to be over 300,000 Christians in Cambodia, which has a population of 17 million with an average age of 26.

2024: This year marks the 50th anniversary of the five missionaries from the Overseas Missionary Fellowship (OMF International) entering Cambodia, invited in by the soon-to-be-martyred Major Taing Chhirc.

Of all the evil Khmer Rouge leaders, only one remains alive: Khieu Samphan, their former Head of State, serving a life sentence for his massive crimes against humanity, now aged 92.

2025: This year marks the baleful 50th anniversary of the fall of Cambodia to the most radical and malign, Chinese-backed, communist Khmer Rouge on 17 April 1975, resulting in the deaths of upwards of two million people (over 25% of the population) from execution, starvation, disease and slave-labour.

The Cambodian church which they so diligently sought to exterminate, continues to grow and expand the life-giving, peace-giving Kingdom of God all across Cambodia's fields, white unto harvest once more.

In the West today, there is a pervasive consent to the notion of moral relativism, a reluctance to admit that absolute evil can and does exist. This makes it especially difficult for some to accept the fact that the Cambodian experience is something far worse than a revolutionary aberration. Rather, it is the deadly logical consequence of an atheistic, man-centred system of values, enforced by fallible human beings with total power, who believe, with Marx, that morality is whatever the powerful define it to be and, with Mao, that power grows from gun barrels.

David Aikman, *TIME*, 31 July, 1978

WHO WE ARE

Dictum Press, based in Oxford, UK, was founded in 2018. We publish books of global worth (biography, history, doctrine, mission, Christian life) including some modern classics. Browse our titles at *dictumpress.com*, or visit our bookstores at *churchbooks.co.uk* (UK) and *goodread.store* (US).

OMF International was founded by James Hudson Taylor in 1865 as the China Inland Mission. We're now a community of over 2,500 workers from 40 countries, serving the church across East Asia, and among East Asian peoples around the world, by bringing the good news of Jesus Christ in all its fullness. We're forward-thinking, gospel-focused, and willing to pursue every avenue to reach East Asians for Jesus.

Visit *omf.org* to find out more. There you can also find your nearest OMF office. Or search for 'OMF International' on Facebook, Twitter or Instagram. Discover more about our work in Cambodia by visiting *omf.org/cambodia*.

'EBOOKS FOR THE GLOBAL CHURCH'

This initiative provides a small library of 16 ebooks of global worth at no cost to Christians in countries where the church has fewer resources, and to students and student workers globally. If that is you, join the throng at *efacglobal.com/books* to view the titles or to download them. (For others: all the books are in Dictum's online bookstores. See p107.)

'Ebooks for the Global Church' was launched jointly by Dictum and EFAC* in 2023. Writers include John Stott, Ajith Fernando, Chris Wright, Don Cormack, Sinclair Ferguson, Joni Eareckson-Tada, Vaughan Roberts, Lindsay Brown, James Philip, Pablo Martinez.

Christians from any tradition are welcome to receive these books. (*Ten Stories* is in the collection.) Translation rights are available. Any enquiries should be sent to Julia Cameron through *dictumpress.com*.

* The Evangelical Fellowship in the Anglican Communion was founded in 1961 by John Stott.